# TRAINING CAMP FOR LIFE

By Steve Sanders

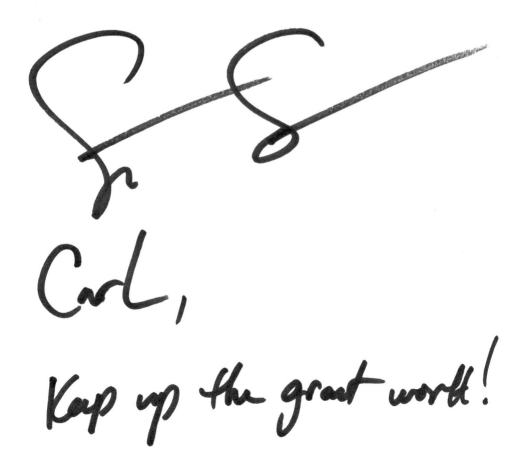

Carl,

Keep up the great work!

Edited by: Jennifer Wainwright

Cover Design: Shannon Wainwright

Interior Layout Design: Shannon Wainwright

Executive Producer: Mirica A. Stevens

Sanders, Steve

Training Camp For Life: Developing Champions In Sports And In Life / Steve Sanders

ISBN-10: 0988428539

ISBN-13: 978-0-9884285-3-9

We hope you enjoy this book from TCFL Publishing. Our goal is to provide high-quality, thought-provoking books and products that are relatable to each reader's needs and challenges. For more information on other books and products written and produced by Steve Sanders and TCFL Publishing, go to www.tcflpublishing.com

Email: publishing@tcflpublishing.com, or write to:
TCFL Publishing
PO Box 602260
Cleveland, Ohio 44102

Printed in the United States of America

# Table of Contents

*This book is dedicated to the millions of young athletes that I **GET** to inspire, impact, and influence!*

*Thank you for allowing me to fulfill my divine assignment in life.*

*Preface*

## THE NEED FOR TRAINING CAMP FOR LIFE

Statistics show less than 1% of athletes make it to the professional stage in their sport of choice yet millions of young athletes have aspirations of living out their dream to make it to the big stage. Due to this fact, Training Camp For Life's immediate target audience is young athletes ages thirteen to twenty-five years old. I understand that every young athlete may not go professional in a sport but potentially they will become college graduates, business owners, husbands, fathers, community leaders, and role models. I challenge myself to prepare them for their futures.

## STATISTICS ON YOUNG ATHLETES

### High School to Pro – How Many Will Go?

- Fifty-nine percent of high school football and basketball players believe they will get a college scholarship.

- Ninety-eight out of one hundred high school athletes never play collegiate sports of any kind at any level.

- Less than one out of every one hundred high school athletes receive a scholarship of any kind to a Division I school.

- Nationally, out of every one hundred ninth graders, sixty-eight will graduate from high school, forty will enter college directly, twenty-seven are still enrolled in college in their second year, and eighteen will graduate from college. These numbers include all students entered in college. - US Department of Education 2011.

- Only one of sixteen thousand high school athletes attain a professional career in sports  - **_less than 1%._**

## Psychographics Description

Lets face it, the demographic of young athletes ages thirteen to twenty-five years old are not buying books off the shelves for leisure reading. Statistically, they purchase books for school; buy sports magazines or read free articles online. Being aware of this information, it is my call to action for adults to support this book by purchasing it for a young athlete. Who should purchase this book? Parents/guardians who want their young athlete(s) to obtain a college scholarship, parents/guardians who are frustrated with their young athlete(s) who put sports above academics, and parents/guardians who wish to become knowledgeable on the issues their young athlete(s) is/are faced with today. In addition, I expand this call to action to high school coaches seeking to get their players a full athletic college scholarship, college coaches who want to keep their players focused on the importance of graduating with a college degree, and coaches looking to help young athletes pursue their dreams of going pro in a sport. Lastly, I ask supporters and sponsors to partner with me by purchasing *Training Camp For Life* books to donate to high schools, colleges, and youth sports organizations throughout the country. This will encourage and inspire young athletes to read more books, ultimately addressing a literacy epidemic across the nation.

# DEVELOPING CHAMPIONS IN SPORTS AND IN LIFE SERIES

*The Training Camp For Life: Developing Champions In Sports And In Life* books are a three-part series. Initially, my plan was to write one book on a multitude of topics. After careful consideration, I realized that 300+ pages in one book probably wouldn't be very appealing to young athletes. So I made the decision to divide the book into a series. Roughly seventy-five to one hundred pages, each book on average is eight to ten chapters in length. This will allow every reader to grasp the concepts I teach without feeling overwhelmed with information. We all know that it becomes very difficult to apply what you learn when you are overwhelmed. My overall mission for this book is to get athletes to emphasize "application." It's one thing to know something, but it is a completely different ball game when it comes to applying what you know to an area of your life.

Maybe it's my fault.

Maybe I led you to believe it was easy when it wasn't.

Maybe I let you think my success is all my doing and not God-given.

Maybe I let you think playing in the NFL was more important than graduating from college.

Maybe I led you to think that you can only make it out of your situation if you play basketball, football, or rap!

Maybe it's my fault that you didn't see my failure gave me strength, that my pain was my motivation.

Maybe I led you to believe that writing this book wasn't the greatest thing I've ever done in my life!

Maybe I destroyed the game... OR
MAYBE...
YOU JUST MAKING EXCUSES!!!

**Steve Sanders,** Inspired by Michael Jordan

# Forethought - Why Training Camp For Life?

I will probably receive more credit for writing this book than I am truly due. The process of penning to paper the lessons and advice I share in this book has been one of the most challenging yet rewarding accomplishments of my life. Although, becoming a published author nowadays isn't as great of an accomplishment compared to the eighties and nineties with the popularity of eBooks and self-publishing.

But for a young man who struggled with reading his entire life, this is huge. For a former NFL player whose career was short-lived, a man who was homeless and sleeping on friends' and family members' couches while he was writing this book, this is more than a big deal; it's nothing short of a testament of God's grace in my life.

Most people don't know that I was reading at a fourth-grade level when I was a junior in college. It wasn't that I didn't have the ability to learn how to read; my pride and attitude hindered me from trying. I credit my college coach and his wife, Zach and Julia Azzani, for helping me to learn to read. If it wasn't for their genuine love for me and the rest of the wide-receiver core at Bowling Green State University, I don't know if I would have ever opened up to anyone about my struggle.

I was homeless after playing a few seasons in the NFL—another thing most people probably don't know about me. I hid the fact that I was destitute. Again, my pride wouldn't allow me to ask for support. My truck was repossessed, my credit was shot, and I was evicted from my place. I had hit rock bottom. Even still, I was in denial. I kept my head high in public, but in private I would cry myself to sleep at night. I was hurting. I was grieving because I felt like a failure in life. At one point I suffered from depression. I remember praying to God to help me. Little did I know, He was helping me.

It was at my lowest point that I rededicated my life to Christ. It was at that time in my life I found my future wife. God placed her in my life at a time when I needed her. Next to my relationship with God, she is the very reason I was able to write this book. Her love, support and affirmation motivated me to pursue my dream of becoming a published author. So to Mirica Stevens, the love of my life and wife to be, thank you, baby!

Although, it was the most difficult period of my life, it was at that time that I began to understand and walk in my purpose in life. I am a true witness that God will take your misery and turn it into your ministry.

So, when people ask "Why *Training Camp For Life*?", I will be able to share with them my incredible journey. I will point to my faith in my Lord and Savior Jesus Christ. It is because of my faith in Him that this book is possible. I was led by His spirit to write every word in this book. It is my sincere prayer that each of you too will allow yourself to be spirit-led to fulfill your God given purpose in life. As you read each chapter take time to reflect on your own life. Ask yourself, "what is God trying to get to me or get done through me?".

*Training Camp For Life: Developing Champions In Sports And In Life* is not considered a Christian book, but I share my faith in this forethought with readers because God is the number one reason I wrote this book.

To the people that supported me physically, mentally, and spiritually throughout the process of this journey, I thank you:

My Son, Armier Sanders
My Mother, Teresa Majors
My Brother, Timothy Majors
My Sister, Twonna Majors and Family
My Best Friend, Marcus Allen and Wife Kim Allen
My Trainer and Friend, Antonio Coleman

.

# INTRO-
# DUCTION

**"Therefore I run in such a way, as not without aim; I box in such a way, as not beating the air; but I discipline my body and make it my slave, so that, after I have preached to others, I myself will not be disqualified."**

– 1 Corinthians 9:26, 27 NASB

Like you and every other person on earth who's lived a little while, I have had a lot of experiences over the course of my life, some good and some bad. Of those significant experiences that I can recall, I found a way to learn from them and use what I learned to my advantage in a future situation. This is not something that I always knew how to do; it's a practice I acquired after making enough mistakes to understand that I needed to consider my actions and behaviors both before and after I made them to mature and grow into the person I wanted to be and to have the most desirable, rewarding life possible.

When I reflect back on some of those experiences, I realize that there were times when I made bad decisions of my accord, and then there were other times where I leaned on someone I trusted for advice and they mistakenly pointed me in the wrong direction. In all cases, my experiences taught me that hindsight is always 20/20. You see things so much more clearly in retrospect, which is one reason why making time for personal reflection is so important.

There is undeniable value in each of our experiences and if we spend the necessary time reflecting after every meaningful experience we have in life, we can learn a lot about ourselves and the world, which can help us grow into purposeful, productive human beings.

*Training Camp For Life* does exactly that for each reader. In this book, I provide you with ways, tools, and examples of how to reflect and capitalize on every opportunity or notable experience you have in life. Whether you're playing in the championship game of your sport, trying to make a team, coaching in high school, or raising young athletes, this book will speak to you on a myriad of topics that can pave the way for your success and possibly even prevent you from making choices that lead to unfavorable consequences.

Throughout this book I offer my personal experiences as conversation starters and a guideline to the topics we will discuss in every chapter. My goal is to inspire you and show you how to use your own daily life experiences to springboard you to the successful outcomes you desire.

Initially, my target audience for this book was young male athletes, partly because my life experiences speak directly to that particular audience. But after I finished writing and reviewing my work, I realized that the information I've shared is useful to an audience beyond young male athletes. This book is also for coaches working with young male athletes, dads, male teachers, male mentors, and any other men that work with young male athletes.

It is no secret that most young male athletes are being raised in single parent homes. The principles in this book can also be very helpful for single moms raising young men, female coaches working with young male athletes, female teachers, any women that spend time with young male athletes, and yes, even, young ladies that find themselves interested in young male athletes. If you want to relate to or identify with a male athlete on one level or another, there is something in here for you.

Oftentimes as the adults working with these young men, we have our own struggles and need advice or guidance in leading them in the right direction. The principles in *Training Camp For Life* will present you with tools that will help you along this sometimes difficult yet fulfilling journey.

*Training Camp For Life – Developing Champions In Sports And In Life* is a three-part series. This is Part I. This book will allow us to begin the process. It is intended to lay the foundation for what we'll address over the course of the entire series. Similar to building a home, the foundation is the most important part of developing a champion in sports and in life.

I'm excited to embark on this journey with you. I hope you're excited too. Let us begin...

# CHAPTER 1

# SO YOU SAY YOU WANT TO BE SUCCESS-FUL?

1

## "Today I will do what others won't, so tomorrow I can accomplish what others can't."

– Jerry Rice (#1 NFL Wide Receiver Of All Time)

In my early years, I made a lot of excuses for my failures and took a lot—if not all—the credit for my successes. My failures were never my own doing. It was always something that happened to me or someone that caused me to fail with their bad advice that I should have never listened to in the first place. That's how I thought at the time.

I took those failures, or perhaps a better rendering might be *bad experiences*, for granted. I didn't understand the value in life's bad experiences or even the value in good experiences for that matter. I didn't realize what I could gain from appreciating those situations and circumstances for what they were, and allowing them to profitably influence the direction of my life. My attitude was "I'm on to the next thing" or "Since it wasn't my fault anyway I'm just going to push that out of my head."

Needless to say, somewhere in my past, I had adopted the wrong mindset about life. I had the attitude of a person who didn't understand success and what it takes to achieve it.

I spent my teenage years and early twenties thinking this way and boy did I pay for it. Everything was someone else's fault. I hardly ever took the blame for my actions and it cost me dearly in many situations. Some of those situations include relationships, houses, vehicles, friendships, a successful NFL career, and even millions of dollars. Man, was I stupid!

Most people will probably share my latter sentiment and that's what I felt like initially reflecting back on my journey. In reality, this happens to almost everyone on a daily basis. We sacrifice or forfeit things and people who are significant to us because we refuse to accept responsibility for our actions or our part in why a particular situation played out the way it did.

Most of us either don't properly diagnose the behavior that leads to failure or we fail to learn from our failures. This type of conduct is called selfishness. It's how selfish individuals think and act. I was one of the most selfish individuals my friends and acquaintances probably knew. Sure, I did a lot things for other people. I donated to charities, read books to kids, and gave back to my community. But I was selfish on the inside. I wanted to reap the benefits from every opportunity but never accept the failures of them. I was too selfish to admit when I had made a mistake along the way somewhere. I was too selfish to stop and reflect on my disappointments and allow them to become learning lessons for me.

"

I allowed my
selfish behavior
and emotional
immaturity to
get the best of me
and reacted poorly
when things
didn't go my
way.

# SO YOU SAY YOU WANT TO BE SUCCESSFUL?

Let me tell you a quick story about one of my most selfish behaviors. Five years ago I played football in the National Football League (NFL). I was what you would call a "rising star." I was playing for my hometown team, the Cleveland Browns, living out my childhood dream in my third season with the club in line to succeed a future hall of famer. The previous two seasons I was a practice squad player. The term *practice squad* is used to describe a player who is on the team only to practice and prepare. You see the real players, the ones that play in the games, on television.

But this was my season. I was finally getting the chance I felt I deserved. At least that's what I thought would happen. The year didn't go anywhere near as I planned. By the end of the year I wanted out of Cleveland. I was sick of being overlooked. I was tired of playing backup to guys everyone knew I was better than. I worked my butt off to get a shot and it still didn't happen for me. I called my agent and told him to get me out of Cleveland. I couldn't take it anymore. My agent didn't agree but I didn't care. So I rejected an offer to resign with Cleveland and signed with the Detroit Lions. The following season, the Browns' coaching staff was fired, the future hall of fame wide receiver I was behind was forced into retirement by a surgery gone wrong, another wide receiver received a yearlong suspension for a DUI that cost a man his life and another was traded because of a bad attitude and declining performance. I couldn't make this up if I tried. Needless to say, I had reacted selfishly and really shot myself in the foot.

Things didn't work out for me in Detroit and after being released prior to the season I signed with the Arizona Cardinals. That too ended in me being released after a short time. All I could think was, *I should have stayed with the Browns.* I allowed my selfish behavior and emotional immaturity to get the best of me and reacted poorly when things didn't go my way. My foolish reaction was part of the reason my NFL career ended. What if I would have stayed in Cleveland? What if I would have stopped and reflected before I made an irrational decision? What if I would have embraced my role as a backup or listened to my agent's expert advice? Would I still be playing in the NFL today? I will never know the answer to that question. But what I do know is my selfish behavior caused me to regret the decisions I made. I do know that if I would've been unselfish I would have taken the time to reflect and listen to counsel prior to making a major decision.

I can't tell you what every successful person does. This isn't a book on the secrets no one else knows about. In fact, many people know about the things I am going to detail throughout this book so they aren't really secrets. You just may not know them at this point in your life.

I don't claim to be an expert on what it takes to make it to the pros or how to win a championship. I am an expert on the areas of work ethic, goal setting, and defining individual success. I am also skilled in developing young athletes and coaches, and advising parents on how to reach and connect with their young athletes.

# SO YOU SAY YOU WANT TO BE SUCCESSFUL?

What makes me an expert? I'm glad you asked. I have over fifteen years of experience in high school, collegiate, and professional sports. Combined with this experience, I am also a certified professional life coach, committed to helping others create winning attitudes in their pursuit of success. My areas of expertise include athletics, leadership, goal setting, and performance training. Lastly, I am currently pursuing a master's degree in sports psychology and will follow that with my Ph.D. shortly thereafter.

This book is the testimony of a person who understands the importance of learning from life's experiences. It is one athlete's journey, an athlete who has ruminated on what he would have done differently if he only understood how to value things earlier in life. This is my personal view on what has led me to success. This is me owning my story and sharing it with you to prevent young male athletes with similar upbringings, goals, and dreams from making similar mistakes. This is my expressed will to propel young male athletes to success through their own triumphs and failures in life. So let's jaywalk straight to it. You say you want to be successful? Let's see how bad you really want it.

# THE DEFINI-TION OF SUCCESS

# 2

**"The call on my life is so much greater than the game of basketball."**

– LeBron James

Before we can explore success, let's first define it. Merriam-Webster's dictionary defines *success* as follows:

1. *Obsolete: outcome, result*

2. *Degree or measure of succeeding*

3. *Favorable or desired outcome; also: the attainment of wealth, favor, or eminence*

4. *One that succeeds*

Webster's does a superb job defining success but for the purposes of this book, we are going to use this working definition: *success is the progressive realization of a worthy idea; if a person is working toward a predetermined goal and knows where they are going, they are a success.*

Success is a difficult word to define due to the fact that success can be measured in many ways. What might be success to a stockbroker is not the same as success for a teacher. Our working definition allows us to generalize success in almost any category. Whether you are a stay-at-home dad or the starting goalie for an NHL team, using this definition, you can achieve success in any way, shape, form, or fashion.

Success can be great if it's achieved the right way. I won't sit here and say that it can't be achieved by cheating your way through the system, because it can be. Despite the cliché "cheaters never win," cheaters win all the time. But what I can tell you is cheaters never prosper. The word *prosper* comes from the word prosperity. Prosperity comes when you are in purpose and purpose is something you can't cheat your way through. Therefore, trying to cheat your way to prosperity is impossible. This is why cheaters never prosper.

The success a person receives from cheating is often unfulfilling. It looks good on the outside but on the inside something is missing. Something is lacking; there is a void or an empty feeling that leaves you wanting more even after you have tasted success. This can be best explained by looking at America's prison system.

Our prisons are full of people who cheated their way to some type of success. Prisons are filled with repeat offenders. Many of those in our prisons are individuals who succeeded at cheating the system at some point in time and when they tried to get away with it again they were caught. In their minds, if they got away with it one time, they can get away with it again, prompting them to go after "success" once more, even at the risk of returning to prison. **Success is not defined by what you achieve but by how you achieved it.**

Now that we have a working definition for success, let's discuss some things you need to know about success.

# SUCCESS IS A CHOICE

Choosing success is optional. Sadly, most people choose not to succeed more often than they choose success. Being successful doesn't come easy to the average person but what it takes to be successful is no secret. To achieve success, you must have mental toughness, stick-to-itiveness, and focus. For those who have experienced success, it is really easy and common. As a matter-of-fact, they expect it. They have adopted a mindset of anticipating that great things will happen to them and for them as long as they employ the three things mentioned above— mental toughness, stick-to-itiveness, and focus.

The reason the unsuccessful stay unsuccessful is that they lack three things: determination, dedication, and discipline, which I refer to as the 3 D's. For the next few paragraphs we will explore the 3 D's and why they are critical to being successful at any and everything you want in life. The faster you master the 3 D's, the faster you can be on your way to becoming a success at multiple things in your life.

## D-Word #1 – Determination

Determination can be summed up as simply setting your mind on something and going after it relentlessly. Before you can be determined to have success you must first decide what it is you're determined to be successful at.

We live in a fast-paced world. We often perceive that things come easy but this view of life is deceptive. Every success starts with a thought, a conscientious decision that is, to go after that success. Making a decision and sticking to it is key.

I know you may be thinking, *I'm young and I don't have life figured out yet*, or, *I'm already out of my prime so why even try at this point?* The great thing about success is that it has no bias. Your age, gender, race, size, nor weight matters. Success awaits all those who are willing to pursue it. So if you're in high school and you think, *I have time to decide what I want in life*, that's not necessarily true. Yes, you have time but not enough time to wait around doing nothing or jumping from thing to thing hoping that something will stick. Your teenage years are a great opportunity to learn stick-to-itiveness. Forming a habit of sticking with things is one of the best habits you'll ever create in your life. The sooner you realize this and develop it, the more likely you are to become successful in life at the things you choose to do. This leads us to the pursuit of success.

After you've decided on what you want to pursue, the next step is creating a plan. It's not enough to just decide to succeed. It is the first step but arguably more important is the next step, the plan for success. I believe the age-old truism, *if you don't plan to succeed, you plan to fail.* You have to know where you're going if you want to succeed.

Let me give you an example. A cruise ship without a captain, crew, or destination will definitely end up shipwrecked, if it even makes it out of the dock. Without a destination, the ship is surely headed for destruction.

Now consider that same cruise ship with a skipper, qualified staff, and exact destination. I think you'll agree that it will almost certainly arrive at its targeted destination (unless it's the Titanic, which I know some smart aleck reader is thinking). But all jokes aside, as in the cruise ship example, you need to have a plan for your navigation. You must know where you're going before you can attempt to be successful on your journey. Creating a plan to be successful is not easy by any means but to help you along this journey, I have provided a free sample downloadable success plan that I have personally used over the years. Visit www.TrainingCampForLife.org and go to our free downloads page. You will find other helpful resources there as well.

Now that you have an idea of a success plan you can begin to write your own; however, you have to be aware of the pitfalls of a success plan. As you embark on your campaign toward success, you will come up against things that will limit your progress, slow your process, or possibly cause you to stop pursuing completely.

## Three things that will kill your success plan:

### 1. *Procrastination*

Procrastinating can wreck your success plan faster than anything else. This is because procrastinating is solely on you. It's self-destruction.

One of the most popular rap artists of this time, Jay Z (AKA Shawn Carter), talks about procrastination in his classic song "Meet the Parents." Describing a situation of hesitation, Jay Z says, "He who hesitates has lost."

Procrastination is the worst form of hesitation. It shows that you lack faith, discipline, and determination. If you want to be successful, you can't afford to procrastinate for long periods of times. We all procrastinate, but postponing your goals for years, months, or even weeks will severely compromise your ability to reach success.

### 2. *Lack of Focus*

The second snare that can hinder your success is a lack of focus. Failing to focus on the plan you've created will keep you stagnant and ultimately lead to you feeling as though your plan doesn't work, causing you to give up and quit altogether.

Focus relates to commitment. Ask yourself, *How committed am I to implementing my plan and succeeding?* In other words, HOW BAD DO YOU WANT IT? If it's success in a sport that you're aiming for, how many additional hours a day are you putting in to improve? Yes, hours per day! Committing to improving in a sport is not something you do every other day or week. It's a daily grind. You have to commit. Whether it's working on your free throws after every practice, going to the batting cage when you'd rather be playing video games, or studying film on an upcoming opponent instead of watching your favorite show, you have to do something to get better and stay focused every single day. There is no such thing as a day off for someone who wants to be successful.  You have to buckle down and be dedicated to focusing on your plan. If not, your lack of focus will allow you to become easily distracted, greatly diminishing any chance you have to achieve your desires.

### 3.  *Unnecessary Distractions*

You must be vigilantly aware of unnecessary distractions. I specify distractions as unnecessary because there are necessary distractions as well. Unnecessary distractions can be defined as things that are not directly related to or that disrupt the flow of your success plan.

Let me give you a few examples: If you're trying to review for a test and your Facebook notifications keep popping up drawing your attention away from your studies, that's an unnecessary distraction. The latest status update from friends who you were probably just with in the last few hours is not necessary for you to ace your test.

On the flipside, a necessary distraction would be your dad telling you to take out the garbage and wash the dishes. There is a big difference in the two scenarios. The second is not something that will help you ace the test but it will keep you from being on punishment for the next few days.

What are some other unnecessary distractions that can potentially kill your success plan? List your top three.

1. _____

2. _____

3. _____

## D-Word #2 – Dedication

After you have determination and know where you are going, the next step is to dedicate yourself to the new success you've set out to accomplish. Your level of dedication will be a major factor in how successful you become. The things we love or want out of life are the things we dedicate ourselves to. When you

"

**Prosperity comes when you are in purpose and purpose is something you can't cheat your way through. Therefore, trying to cheat your way to prosperity is impossible. This is why cheaters never prosper.**

want something with all your heart, you'll dedicate yourself to it and go after it nonstop until you achieve it. Your level of dedication will depend on your ability to focus. Why is focusing so important? I'm glad you asked! Focusing on your success (or not) dictates your outcome, and here are a few reasons why:

1. *Your focus will determine the amount of energy you put toward succeeding.*

Focus requires energy. The type of energy your focus requires depends on the kind of task or challenge you're facing. It may be mental, physical, or spiritual energy, or even a combination of the three. If you're positively focused on something you're bringing an enormous amount of energy toward it. That energy doesn't get wasted. It goes into everything you do to become successful. Your determination, dedication, and discipline all make up this energy, ultimately propelling you in the direction of success that you desire.

2. *Your focus will help you avoid the pitfalls that will prevent you from succeeding.*

Pitfalls are situations that cause you to stay stuck. They are harmful situations that put you at a disadvantage and require a lot of time and energy to get out of. You've probably experienced some pitfalls of your own, and if you haven't, keep on living and you'll come across your fair share.

Pitfalls are traps, often hidden, and if you're not focused on what you need to do, they can easily dupe or deceive you. They are designed to catch you up, set you up, and mess you up. Successful athletes and celebrities deal with pitfalls more than anyone. Here's why: being a successful athlete comes with a lot of attention, recognition, and fame, which is not necessarily bad. As a matter-of-fact, becoming famous and receiving lots of attention can open up many opportunities for you to change lives and support worthy causes. Sadly, many people take advantage of their popularity in negative ways as well.

Using your popularity in a harmful way is the ultimate pitfall to avoid. Wanting to become successful for money, fame, acceptance, and/or women will have you broke, busted, and disgusted. I'm not telling you what I think, I'm telling you what I know.

I was a victim of the athlete/celebrity pitfall. I loved to be in the spotlight. I thrived off the attention and I loved the women. I got everything I wanted, everyone knew my name, and I was loved by more than I was hated by. But the more attention I got the more attention I wanted. The more women I got, the more women I wanted. Nothing satisfied me and after a while I wondered why. My appetite kept increasing but I could never satiate it. I was empty. Even after nights that seemed to be full of fun and adventure, I was dissatisfied. Something was missing and I felt it.

As I share my story with you throughout this book, it's not to boast or brag about what I have or had. I want to save you from making some of the stupid, immature mistakes I made out of ignorance during my career as an athlete and as a young man. It boils down to this: if you're not careful with all that comes with a profitable career, your success can become your worst enemy, stripping every important, meaningful thing and person from your life and leaving you wondering what happened.

Women, the overwhelming love for money, materialistic behavior, the wrong attention for the wrong reasons, bad attitudes, lack of respect for authority and coaches, deceit, and distrust are just a few pitfalls athletes deal with that compromise your focus very quickly.

3. *Your focus will help guard you against self-inflicted wounds.*

Avoiding pitfalls may not be hard for you but something we all deal with is self-inflicted wounds. I'm not speaking of physically harming or damaging your body but rather those avoidable, unnecessary situations that you personally prompted.

Self-inflicted wounds are unique to every situation. If you're trying to stay focused on eating right, a self-inflicted wound would be going to the store and purchasing junk food. You know you're trying to improve your performance and you DECIDED not to eat junk food, yet you buy it from the store only to tell yourself, "I'm not going to eat it." Yeah, **sure** you won't!

Your vice, whatever it is, will limit your progress and reduce your focus. STAY AWAY FROM IT! If you want to be in a committed relationship with a young lady you like you're going to have to delete the numbers of all the girls you used to talk to, defriend them on Facebook, unfollow all the pretty girls you've been following on Instagram and Twitter and stop flirting with every girl you see that has a nice shape and pretty face. That's just real. It may sound like a lot to do but the question is, how bad do you want to be with this young lady you like? I've gone as far as deleting all of my personal social media sites to make a relationship work because I wanted someone that bad.

It comes down to a simple question. What are you doing that is compromising your focus that can be avoided? If you're committed to taking your studies seriously, what is keeping you from putting more time in? If it's sports, what's holding you back from excelling to the next level? If it's commitment, what are you afraid of? Ask yourself these questions and be honest in answering them. It's only going to help you. Leaving self-inflicted wounds unaddressed won't make them go away. In fact, they will only get worse and you'll keep getting yourself caught up in the same situations over and over and over again throughout life. Eliminate your self-inflicted wounds and watch your life start to flourish in that particular area.

What are some of the self-inflicted wounds limiting you from achieving the success you desire in different areas of your life?

List your top three:

1. _____

2. _____

3. _____

## D-Word #3 – Discipline

Now that you have determination and dedication, it's time to get disciplined. This is probably the most important 'D' word yet. You have to have discipline to achieve anything in life. Without discipline, determination and dedication can't exist.

Discipline is what you will need to reap the benefits of all the hard work, determination, and dedication you've put in. For us athletes, discipline is vital. Our discipline has to be great in our desired sport. An example of discipline comes to mind when I think of training and practice. When you're working out and no one else is watching or counting, do you cheat on your reps? When you're running sprints do you finish strong and run through the line or do you ease up and coast the last few steps? This is discipline at its best. What do you do when no one else is watching?

Discipline is giving up the temporary victory or feeling for the ultimate prize. If it's a sport, we are talking about winning the game or a championship. If it's a committed relationship, we are talking about finding the woman of your dreams and marrying her. If it's in the classroom, we are talking averaging a 3.0 GPA or better on any level. Whatever the ultimate goal is, self-discipline will separate you from the rest. It's easy to see who has it. Everyone can tell, because those individuals stand out. Having self-discipline alone will not guarantee your success, but not having self-discipline is the one thing that will guarantee your failure.

**What does self-discipline do for you?**

1. Self-discipline separates you from the crowd. If you want to stand out, do it for the right reasons and do things the right way. Self-discipline will set you apart because most people lack restraint in multiple areas of their lives.

2. Self-discipline helps to further eliminate distractions. There is that word again, *distractions*. You will hear it a lot throughout this book. Eliminate distractions and eliminate distracting failures.

# SUCCESS IS A PROCESS, NOT AN END RESULT

# 3

# SUCCESS IS A PROCESS, NOT AN END RESULT

**"I've missed more than 9,000 shots in my career. I've lost almost 300 games. Twenty-six times, I've been trusted to take the game winning shot and missed. I've failed over and over and over again in my life. And that is why I succeed…"**

– Michael Jordan (Greatest NBA Basketball Player Of All Time)

Most people who hear the word *success* hear achievement or completion as well. The fact is, much of the success you have in life will go unnoticed by most people because they don't know that success is a process, not an end result. Sure, it feels good to achieve success and reap the benefits you've worked so hard to get but the real success is in the amount of time and effort you put into achieving that success. It's about the commitment, dedication, determination, and discipline you put into it.

When you focus enough to overcome obstacles and pitfalls and can look back and say, "I did it," what you will remember the most is not the success itself, but the process it took to get there.

I don't know what your desired success is, but I do know that you'll feel so much better when you get there knowing that you earned it. You'll appreciate it more. And by going through the process, you'll know just what it takes to achieve that success, and then you can mimic those steps to become successful in another area of your life.

The process of success doesn't come easy by any means. There will be ups and downs, smiles and frowns, tears of pain and tears of joy, but through it all you will know that no matter what, you stuck with it and you have your success to show for it.

When an NBA or NFL team wins the Finals or a Super Bowl championship, one of the first things you'll hear them say is, "We've come a long way." What they're saying is, "We've endured the process." In sports, the championship is complete when you hold up that trophy, but the road to get there begins in training camp. It started when the previous season ended and you told yourself you were going to work harder so your team could win the next year and be crowned champions.

Winning a championship is a great feeling and something that can never be taken away from you if you've earned it because you put in the blood, sweat, and tears it took to win. The same thing applies in life. Especially for men. When we set out to accomplish something and do it, there is no greater feeling. Success is something you earn, it's not given to you. If it is, it's probably not success; by definition, it's a gift, and can be taken away from you at some point.

Set your eyes on everlasting success that you own because you earned it. When you do this, you'll feel the joyful emotion of true triumph, something only a few have an opportunity to feel because only a few endure the process it takes to get there.

# SUCCESS DOESN'T HAPPEN BY ACCIDENT; IT'S PLANNED

I attended Bowling Green State University where I played five seasons. The first two of those seasons I played for a great coach by the name of Urban Meyer. You may or may not know him. Urban Meyer is one of the most winningest coaches in college football history. He has won 2 BCS National Championships, had 2 undefeated seasons, and has over 125 wins as a head coach throughout his career.

Before all the wins and BCS Championships, Coach Meyer started his head coaching career at BGSU. I remember sitting in the team huddles after practice listening to him as a freshman. He would say things like, "We don't win by accident," and "How bad do you want it?" And my favorite, "Why not us? Why not now?"

Coach Meyer was an excellent motivator. He knew just what to say to get his team fired up and ready to go. But his motto "We don't win by accident" was not just motivational speak, it was true. That stuck with me throughout my football career and carried over into my life. Coach Meyer used it to motivate us to practice hard and give all we had every day we stepped out onto the field. Today I use it to explain how to achieve success in your life.

Success doesn't just stroll down the block, tap you on the shoulder and say, "I pick you." Sadly, you can walk up and down the street today and see people that think that's what will happen to them. Waiting for success is what I call it. Why are you waiting for success? Success doesn't wait on you. Success goes to anyone who gets up and gets it. Just as Coach Meyer would tell us, "I can't promise you that you'll go pro but I can promise you if you do what is asked of you and give all you have, you'll win." Not only will you win in athletics, but you'll win at life, the ultimate game we play every day.

Yesterday is gone and tomorrow isn't promised. Now is the time to start planning for success. Don't put off what you can do today for tomorrow. The sooner you start planning for success the sooner the process starts.

## SUCCESS = SACRIFICE

Another word for success is sacrifice. If you want to be successful you're going to have to sacrifice some things. Let me tell you a story I once heard, a story about how monkeys are caught in Africa.

"

**Success doesn't wait on you. Success goes to anyone who gets up and gets it.**

# SUCCESS IS A PROCESS, NOT AN END RESULT

In Africa, monkey catchers bait their prey using coconut shells and peanuts. Sounds weird but let me explain before you start laughing. They cut a small hole in the coconut that's just big enough for a monkey to put his hand through. Then, they put peanuts in the bottom of the coconut. Next, they tie a string to it and hide. When the monkey comes along to get the peanuts, he sticks his hand in the coconut and grabs the peanuts. The monkey catcher then pulls the string and pulls the monkey to him. The monkey can get away if he chooses to but the only way to do so is to SACRIFICE the peanuts he wants so badly. If he opens his fist and lets the peanuts go he can run away and go back to swinging his life away. But more often than not, the monkey doesn't let go and gets himself captured.

Now, I know you aren't a monkey, neither am I implying you are as foolish as the monkeys who get captured. But there is a great comparison to be made here. Success is just as narrow as the hole in the coconut and we can only get through the hole if we SACRIFICE what won't fit. There are some things that we try to hold on to in our lives that we have to let go of. If we only let go of it, we can continue on our journey of success. But we don't. We hold on to it and we get captured, not by a monkey catcher of course, but by failure.

People fail time and time again because they won't sacrifice the things that are holding them back. What or who is holding you back that you won't let go of? What areas of your life are you trying to pull out of but can't because your hands are full? Have you ever seen someone in the airport at the check-in counter with overweight luggage? It's funny but sad when you think of it. Instead of paying the fee for overweight luggage they start to shift things around from bag to bag. I call this the balancing act. They take the bag that is heaviest and shift things from that bag to a bag that has less weight. So why don't they just pay the fee? Good question.

Most people can't afford the higher fees associated with heavier luggage. Others just refuse to pay them because the cost is ridiculously high. This is a perfect parallel to success. You're at the check-in counter of success and your bags are overweight. Will you sacrifice and pay the price success wants for your extra baggage? Will you play the balancing act and try to shift things from bag to bag? Or will you refuse to pay the high cost associated with getting on the plane of success and just not go? These are all questions I pose to you in a joking manner but sacrificing for success is no joking matter.

# THE COST OF SUCCESS

# 4

**"It's not the will to win that matters—everyone has that. It's the will to prepare to win that matters."**

- Paul "Bear" Bryant (Legendary College Football Coach)

There is a cost for success you can't avoid and it's called sacrifice. You either pay it or you don't. Everyone and everything can't go with you on the road to success. Some things have to go. Do a self-evaluation. Ask yourself, *what is holding me back from achieving the success I desire?* Below are five things you may want to consider sacrificing that you aren't aware of:

1.  *Old friends*

We all love our friends and never want to separate from them but sometimes we have to let a friendship go if it's limiting our growth and progress toward success. Letting go of friends is one of the hardest things you'll have to do but the hardest thing to do is usually the best thing to do. Evaluate your friendships to see which ones are holding you back from achieving the success you're pursuing.

2.  *Temporary satisfaction*

This sacrifice goes back to self-discipline. As I mentioned earlier, self-discipline plays a great role in a lot of areas in your life, personally and as it relates to your athletics. Temporary satisfaction feels great when you get it but oftentimes it fades and you're left with nothing or less than you had previously. Sacrifice temporary feelings for lasting ones. You'll be happy you waited; it's worth it.

3. *Fast results*

We live in a world that is fast paced. Everyone is going after short-term victories but expecting long-term results. This isn't how it works. Things that come fast rarely last. If it came quick it's probably going to leave just as quickly. If you spend your time chasing after fast results you're probably going to miss out on your best opportunities for success.

4. *Wants*

Regularly consider your wants versus your needs. What is it that you want? If you really want something, you'll wait for it. If you can't wait for it, it's probably something you don't really need, which brings me to my next question, what is it that you need? Your needs outweigh your wants but it won't seem that way if you don't sacrifice your wants. You can't afford to act like a spoiled kid in a store rolling around on the floor kicking and screaming, "I want it, I want it, I want it." In this situation, success is your mother looking at you like you're crazy waiting for you to tire yourself out. Success doesn't care what you want, only what you need.

5. *Family*

Why sacrifice family? It sounds crazy, but family members can be some of the greatest challenges holding you back from achieving great success in your life. I'm not telling you to cut all ties with your family or distance yourself completely from them, but you do need to set some boundaries.

If you come from a family that's really close and spends a lot of time together, this may be your sacrifice. Hanging out with family is wonderful; continue to do so. But know that when it's time to focus, both you and your family have to acknowledge and respect the boundaries you've set.

Family can be supportive at times but can be enabling at other times. If the family is having a cookout and you have a big test coming that you have to study for, be OK with telling them you can't make it. Of course, they will be disappointed; they love you. But they will respect you more for your discipline and tunnel vision.

# SUCCESS IS INDIVIDUAL

Success comes in all types of ways, and it's specific to the person pursuing it. Therefore, success is what you make it, what you want it to be. Whether it's a small success or great success, success is success. Enjoy it, appreciate it, and value it because you earned it.

Your success is not the next person's success. The work, time, and effort you put into achieving what you set out to achieve is priceless to you. You set the value of your success, not anyone else. The same goes for the success of others. If someone else appears to be reaching success faster or more often than you, don't get discouraged. Stay focused on what you need to do.

You may have heard of the phrase "keeping up with the Joneses." This phrase is used to describe people who try to keep up with what the crowd is doing. If you want to achieve success and continue to achieve it throughout your life, learn quickly that trying to keep up with what everyone else is doing will drive you crazy and lead you straight to failure. This is easier said than done, especially for young people in this day and age because of social media. Anyone can present themselves to be someone who they are not by posting a picture or updating a status. Don't fall for that. This is why I say social media can be a distraction if you allow it to be.

If you find yourself getting caught up in the social media hurricane, get out as fast as you can. Delete your sites and run the opposite way. If deleting your sites is too extreme for you, put yourself on a strict social media schedule. Here's an example of what I mean:

"

**Whether it's a small success or great success, success is success. Enjoy it, appreciate it, and value it because you earned it.**

# THE COST OF SUCCESS

*Log out of your sites*

Log out every time you're done using a site, even on your cell phone. This will limit the amount of your attention your social sites consume daily. We all know that notifications pop up all day long and will distract you from accomplishing daily tasks. If you begin to fall behind on a daily task, how can you achieve your desired success? Social sites are not bad. Keep your pages but don't allow them to eat up all your time. Control your social media presence; don't allow it to control you.

*Control the messages you post*

Control the messages you post on your site. One of the great things about social media is that you manage it. You are your own publicist, promoter, and manager. The message you portray is strictly up to you. This might sound over the top to you now but whether you know it or not employers are observing your social media sites when you apply for jobs. Colleges are doing the same now as well. You don't want to be denied an opportunity because of what you posted on Facebook. Is that post or picture really worth it?

Be smart. Before you post something ask yourself, *is this something I will regret later?* Many of you are thinking, *I'll just delete anything negative I've posted.* Well, keep in mind everything you put on the Internet is written in permanent ink. You can delete a post or picture but it's all archived. You might be able to delete it but you can't erase it. If you plan on becoming a professional athlete you especially need to have good judgment when it comes to your social sites. How many times have you turned on ESPN and saw a commentator talking about a message some popular athlete posted on Twitter? Social media sites are used against athletes all the time. Be the type of athlete who uses his site for positivity, outreach, and motivation to all of their followers, not an athlete who uses it for the exact opposite.

*Stay away from your sites when you're emotional*

Try not to post to your sites when you're emotional. Emotional posts always get you in trouble. If you're upset at something someone did to you, something that happened in class, or about a relationship issue, don't log onto your social media site and rant. First, it's just not a good look. It says that you want attention, and trust me, this isn't the type of attention you want. Second, reacting out of negative emotions always ends in you regretting what you posted and trying to delete it. If you think long and hard before you post something it's likely that you will make better decisions when it comes to what you feel is post-worthy.

You have to stay focused. I challenge you to create your own success, not someone else's. I've given you a lot of things to avoid for individual success but I haven't told you what to do to create it. Let's explore that next.

# HOW TO CREATE INDIVIDUAL SUCCESS

# 5

## "You miss 100 percent of the shots you don't take."

– Wayne Gretzky

To create individual success in your life, you must:

**Live up to your own expectations, not the expectations others have set for you.**

As you go through life, or as I like to say "grow through life," you will experience the pressures of expectations. Expectations are not your enemy. In fact, expectations can be your friend, but you have to be careful or you will potentially allow expectations to overwhelm you. Others will begin to expect things from you or set expectations for you to live up to. Meeting an expectation is not worth your peace, health, or prosperity. Whether it's at school, in a relationship, at home, or on your sports team, expectations will begin to become a part of your life. These types of expectations are OK. Later on in the book I will show you how the devastation of expectations impact our lives.

Set expectations for yourself. Expect more of yourself than anyone else does of you. Be your own worst critic and your own biggest cheerleader. Understanding and knowing what you expect of yourself will allow you to stay focused on what you are trying to accomplish.

When you set expectations for yourself you will notice that most of the time, the expectations of others are met within your own. For example, when the summer job you apply for asks you to write down your top three strengths and top three weaknesses, you will be able to jot them down without racking your brain because you have already identified what they are. Or, when your parents ask you what you have planned for this summer, you can impress them by handing them an itinerary of what you expect to get accomplished because you've already thought it through and mapped it out.

Expectation is all about management. Take some time to write down your own expectations and do your best to live up to them.

What are your expectations in sports?

_____

_____

_____

_____

"

**Being defeated is a temporary condition. Giving up is what makes it permanent.**

What are your expectations at school?

_____

_____

_____

_____

The greatest enemy of success is your fear of failure. If you are going to fail, fail BIG! If you fail at something small people are going to laugh at you anyway.

I measure success by the completion and the fulfillment of the original intent of purpose in your life.

How do you measure success?

_____

_____

_____

_____

You have to master something. Don't be a jack of all trades and master of nothing. You can be good at a lot of things but what are you great at? That's the number one question you must ask yourself if you want to become successful at something: *what can I be great at?*

As you mature throughout life you'll find that things may not always go your way but I want you to always remember this quote by our great president Barack Obama, before he was President of the United States of America. He said, "Being defeated is a temporary condition. Giving up is what makes it permanent." As long as you never give up you will always have an opportunity to become successful along your journey.

CHAPTER 6

# SET YOUR EYES ON THE PRIZE

# 6

**Do you not know that those who run in a race all run, but only one receives the prize? Run in such a way that you may win.**

- 1 Corinthians 9:24 NASB

Ever since I can remember I wanted to play football in the NFL. I was about six or seven years old when my older brother Tim sat me in front of the TV to watch my first football game. Ironically, it was the Browns versus Steelers. I didn't know it at the time but I was watching one of the biggest rivalry games in the NFL.

My brother was a Steelers fan. He sat there with a Terry Bradshaw jersey on in a lazy boy recliner cheering for the gold and black. So being the annoying little brother I was, I decided to cheer for the orange and brown team. It was only right to get back at him for making me watch a football game when I could have been out playing Hide and Go Seek with all my other friends.

The longer we watched the game, the more interested I became. With every play, my excitement intensified. I can still remember seeing #21 for the Browns score touchdown after touchdown. I came to know his name well, Eric Metcalf. The Browns ended up winning the game on an Eric Metcalf punt return for a touchdown. My brother was upset and I didn't make it any better; I cheered as loudly as I could for the Browns. He was so upset he kicked me out of the house. I really didn't care because I had discovered something new—a game called football. I wanted to play right away and imitate Eric Metcalf.

I hurried outside and rounded up all my friends to play a game. I didn't know many rules so we made them up as we went. I had everyone pick a player to be. Of course, I was #21. That's when I set my eyes on the prize of becoming an NFL player. I wanted to be Eric Metcalf from that day forward and play for the Cleveland Browns, and nothing was going to stop me from doing it.

Accomplishing a childhood dream is one of the greatest feelings a person can enjoy and I hope every young person reading this book has the opportunity to feel that joy. There is something inside of every child that makes him or her want to be something special. Whether it's wanting to be a doctor, teacher, fireman, policeman, or astronaut, everyone wants to be something. My question to you is, what do you want to be? What do you want to become when you grow up? What career do you want to pursue? What professional aspirations do you have? These are all questions that I'm sure you've thought of at some point, and if you haven't, now is the time to do so.

Most of you have some type of dream. Something you want to become. If you haven't identified your dream yet, don't feel bad about it. It is my goal that at the end of each chapter you will be a little closer to realizing, planning, and/or accomplishing your dreams.

As you set your eyes ahead on the future there are some key things you'll need to know about achieving your dreams. After you've set your eyes on the prize, you'll need to start setting goals, or benchmarks, to define your journey.

Setting goals is something every successful person does. You may see a person's success but nine times out of ten, you didn't see the process they went through to achieve that success. Setting goals is imperative to achieving anything and everything you want in life. To sum it up, plan to succeed or plan to fail.

Before we discuss how to set goals and accomplish them I want to define what goals are. A goal is defined by Webster's dictionary as:

1. *The result or achievement toward which effort is directed; aim; end*

2. *The purpose toward which an endeavor is directed; an objective*

3. *An observable and measurable end result having one or more objectives to be achieved within a more or less fixed timeframe*

Once again, for the purpose of this book we are going to take Webster's definitions and create a working definition. Our working definition for the word goal is the result of deciding what you want to accomplish and devising (preparing, creating, developing) a plan to achieve the outcome you desire.

## Set S.M.A.R.T. Goals

S.M.A.R.T. is a popular acronym (abbreviation) used to describe a type of goal. I've put my own little twist on the acronym and made it more applicable for you to understand. S.M.A.R.T stands for:

Specific – Be specific in what goal you're trying to accomplish. If you really want to achieve a goal, it is absolutely critical that you be specific and know what you want.

Measurable – Have a way of measuring how successful you are in accomplishing your goals. I will provide you with ways to measure and track your goals later in the next chapter.

Achievable – Make sure that your goals are achievable. Understanding the time commitment and sacrifice will be key in making sure that your goals are attainable. Setting achievable goals can be a challenge at times. Depending on your situation, you want goals that challenge you but you don't want them to be so challenging that you aren't able to maintain them.

Realistic – Along with being achievable you want your goals to be realistic. Realistic goals are unique to every situation. What's

"

**There is something inside of every child that makes him or her want to be something special.**

realistic to some may not be realistic to others, and what's realistic at one time in your life may not be realistic at another time. Remember, whatever goal you set, you will be the only one living up to it or suffering the consequences or failures from it.

Time-based – Every goal should be time-based, that is, you need to have a timeframe that identifies when you plan to have your goal accomplished. Timelines are set based on the type of goal you're trying to achieve. They keep you on task and give you a gauge to measure how much more work needs to go into accomplishing the goal you have set.

**Goals Don't Happen By Accident Either**

Just as I previously explained about success, goals are earned by those who work to achieve them. They aren't given to you by any means. Every goal you want to achieve, every dream of yours that you want to come true will happen because you put in hard work, necessary time, and considerable effort to see that goal or dream come true.

## Goals Come And Go

As you mature into adulthood, you'll see the necessity of setting goals. Some you will accomplish, some you won't, but don't let failed goals discourage you. A failed goal is an opportunity to learn from your mistakes and can be the catalyst that thrusts you into successful goals in the future, as long as you learn from whatever mistakes you made.

Based on my experience, most people don't achieve their goals because they don't set S.MA.R.T. goals, are unknowledgeable about how to properly plan goals, or simply quit when the goal becomes difficult. After reading this chapter you will be equipped with tools to help you set goals properly to ensure that you accomplish them.

## Why Set Goals?

Ever so often I sit back and I think about what I want to be different in my life. I've spent countless hours over the years thinking of things I wanted to accomplish. Whether it was seeing myself as a NFL superstar, multimillionaire philanthropist, or great father, I am always thinking of something and some way to take my life to the next level.

As I set goal after goal, I noticed that I would successfully accomplish some but not others. There had to be a clear-cut reason why, so I began to analyze the goals I set. What distinguished the goals I achieved from the ones I didn't? How were my accomplished goals better or different?

After some extensive evaluation, I began to see a pattern. The goals I set weren't the issue; it was my approach to achieving them, or lack thereof. It took some time but I finally figured it out. I developed a strategy that would allow me to realize almost any goal I am supposed to accomplish and I'm going to share it with you.

It doesn't matter how young or old you are. Your goals can be met if you plan properly and strategize to achieve the outcome you desire. I have been blessed to sit under the tutelage of a wonderful man, my pastor, Dr. R. A. Vernon, Founder and Senior Pastor of "THE WORD" Church in Cleveland, Ohio. He said something that changed my life and I use it all the time now, "You will live at the level you've been taught." That statement is so powerful and true. How can you learn what you haven't been taught? How can you grow in a particular area if you haven't been nurtured in that area of your life? Do you leave it up to chance or just learn by failing time and time again?

My goal for the next chapter is to teach you how to set goals and accomplish them. I want each person reading this to live at a higher level. You will be able to use the plan I give you for every goal you have in any aspect of your life, so let's get right to it.

# CHAPTER 7

# HOW TO SET GOALS & ACCOMPLISH THEM

# 7

## "Set your goals high, and don't stop till you get there."

– Bo Jackson (NFL Legendary Running Back and 2 Sport All-Star (MLB))

Why are people unsuccessful at their goals? Why do some succeed and others fail at accomplishing goals? Why is January 1st of every year full of the same New Year's resolutions people set last January 1st? It's because they don't plan properly, they're using an ineffective strategy, or both.

Before I empower you with ways to set and accomplish any goal you want to achieve, I'd like to tell you a story.

Two ships set sail at the same time. The ships appeared to be the same on the exterior, but there were some major differences in the ships not apparent by simply looking at them.

One ship had a captain and the other ship didn't. The ship with the captain knew where it was going and the captain knew how to get there. He knew what to avoid, how fast to go, and when he needed to slow down. He had a well-trained crew who could help him along the journey to his destination. He knew the cargo he was carrying was valuable and if he stayed the course he would get to his destination just as he planned.

The ship without a captain was a little different. This ship had no idea how it was going to get to its destination. Even though it was set to head in a certain direction it couldn't leave the dock because it had no guidance. Who was going to start the engine? Who would direct the course? Without a captain to lead the plan for the journey this ship would surely crash and never make it to its desired destination.

I shared that story because I want you to understand that you are the captain and your goal is the ship. You have to guide it and understand the value of what you are carrying. Remember, if you don't plan to succeed you plan to fail. Therefore, if you don't have a plan for how you will achieve your goals you might as well be the ship without a captain.

Learning to properly set goals will help you in every aspect of your life. When I say every aspect, I mean every aspect. Whether it's in your career, finances, relationships, education, friendships, or home life, this guide I provide you with can help.

Over the past few years of my life I have read several books on goal setting. Through my research and life experiences I have developed a comprehensive goal-setting guide that will work for anyone of any age, profession, or maturity level. Before I provide you with this guide I need to share with you five benefits of goal setting:

# HOW TO SET GOALS AND ACCOMPLISH THEM

1. *You will achieve more in your life*

2. *You will improve your performances in life*

3. *You will gain motivation to achieve more for your life*

4. *You will experience an increase in your self-confidence*

5. *You will eliminate negative attitudes that hold you back in life*

As you get older, you will begin to understand the patterns you typically follow. Some people establish bad patterns and they see a cycle of the effects play out in their lives. Maybe you're an eighth grader reading this or maybe you're heading to college. I'm not sure what point you're at in your life but I can assure you that it's not too early nor too late for you to get on the right path. Become skilled at goal-setting now and give yourself an advantage. I have learned through my research that people who use goal-setting effectively:

1. *Experience less stress and anxiety*

2. *Concentrate and focus better*

3. *Express more self-confidence*

4. *Perform better in all areas of life*

## Goal Setting Also Helps Self-Confidence

By setting goals, and measuring your goal achievement, you are able to see what you have done and what you are capable of. The process of achieving goals and envisioning yourself achieve your goals will give you confidence in yourself. You have to believe that you can do it. Once I teach you the necessary self-discipline to achieve any goal you set, goal setting will become relatively easy.

This guide is simple and straight to the point, which is why it works. Oftentimes we think complex or difficult means better. But that's not true at all. Sometimes we just need to simplify things. A great acronym I live by is K.I.S.S. – Keep It Simple Stubborn. We can be very stubborn at times, which may cause us to try too hard or be too deep. Just keep it simple. Simple = Successful. Whenever you set a goal from now on, remember to K.I.S.S.

## Why Do People With Goals Succeed?

People with goals succeed because they know where they are going. Some say they have the "magic touch" or "that everything they touch turns to gold." Remember, our working definition for goal is the result of deciding what you want to accomplish and devising a plan to achieve the outcome you desire.

"

**People with goals succeed because they have a plan, not because they are lucky or have something special about them that you don't.**

# HOW TO SET GOALS AND ACCOMPLISH THEM

People with goals succeed because they have a plan, not because they are lucky or have something special about them that you don't. You have the same capability in you, you just haven't been taught how to develop a plan. Well, that is all about to change, right now. I am going to provide you with a goal-setting guide that you will be able to use in any and every aspect of your life.

After you use this plan and succeed at achieving your goals you'll understand what I have been emphasizing to you about the importance of goal setting because you will be one of those successful people I've been talking about. Drum roll, please... Here it is, your goal-setting guide to achieve all of your dreams.

# CHAPTER 8

# TRAINING CAMP FOR LIFE'S GOAL-SETTING GUIDE

**"Talent is God-given. Be humble. Fame is man-given. Be grateful. Conceit is self-given. Be careful."**

– John Wooden (One of the Greatest College Basketball Coaches Of All Time)

## How To Begin Goal Setting:

**Decide** – The first thing need to do is decide what you want and why you want it. Ask yourself some questions like, *what do I want to become?* Or, *where do I see myself in five years?* This will get you started and the answers to the questions you start with will tell you what goals you'll need to set for yourself. Choose goals that put a smile on your face when you think about them. Why would you want to set goals that make you sad? Staying positive is key in accomplishing every goal you set.

**Organize** – Now that you have decided what you want to accomplish, you need to organize your thoughts. Before this point your goals were just ideas. They don't become goals until you organize and plan them out. This takes a little strategy. Organizing is a skill that some people have but many others don't. I don't want to assume you know how to organize your thoughts, so here is a quick way to help you learn how to bring your ideas together so they have some structure.

- Write down all the things you want to accomplish.

- Take the most important things in that list and make a new list; do the same for the least important things.

- At this point, you have two lists. Now take each list and remove what may be least important or unnecessary. If everything is important and necessary keep everything on each list.

- Using a pen and some paper, your iPad, or whatever you use to take notes, create a timeline. Write down one month, three months, six months, one year, three years, and five years. I suggest you only go up to five years to start. You don't want to overwhelm yourself.

**Internalize** – Now that you have organized your thoughts you will need to dig a little deeper. Look inward and ask yourself, *why do I want to achieve this goal? What will it mean to complete it? How will I feel once I accomplish it?* Let your imagination blitz you with reasons and possibilities. In other words, don't limit your answers; be open. Allow your mind to soar when you think of why you have certain goals and all the benefits that will come with achieving them. Oftentimes, thinking of the end result is what pushes us.

I'm not sure what your goals are but whatever they are, begin to feel as though you've already accomplished them. If it's making it to the pros, believe you're there already. Maybe it's graduating from college. If it is, visualize yourself walking across that stage. No matter what your goal is, think, believe, and feel that you've already accomplished it.

Now that you've looked internally, let's get back to your two lists, starting with the important list. I call it your important list, but this could also be your major goals list or long-term goals list. Here's what you do:

- Take the important/major list and place each goal under the area they connect to in your timeline. If this goal is something you can or want to accomplish in one month, place it under the one month column you created. Do this for all the goals you have in the list.

- Repeat the same steps for your least important/short-term goals.

Now your goals are all organized in categories and have timelines attached to them.

**Test** – Now it's time to test what we've covered so far. I want you to find the shortest goal you have and follow the script we've laid out thus far. Decide on a goal, organize the goal, and internalize the goal. You'll be amazed at the immediate results you achieve.

What you just did to begin your goal-setting practice is called *DO IT.* I titled it that because sometimes you just have to DO IT! Start working toward your goals using the instructions outlined here and see what happens. Many times, starting can be the hardest part of doing something. You'll see that once you start goal setting, it will become easier and easier allowing you to build the momentum you'll need on your journey to achieving your dreams.

**State each goal as a positive statement** - Expressing your goals by articulating them in the form of a positive statement is key to you achieving them. This is a powerful and often overlooked step in goal setting. You have to believe that you will achieve the goals you have set for yourself. If you really don't believe, the likelihood of you achieving them is pretty low. When you were deciding what goals you wanted to achieve, I told you to choose goals that made you smile. Now that you are smiling when you think of them, let's act as though you have already reached them. Here are personal examples of how I write my goals down:

- I will be a famous author and inspirational speaker to millions of teens, parents, and coaches.

- I will be a multimillionaire philanthropist who gives millions of dollars to charity.

- I will be a great husband and father.

Whatever your goals are, write them in a positive statement. Use phrases like "I will," "I am," and "I have." Be confident in what you aim to accomplish and the chances of you achieving your goals will be higher.

**Write Your Goals Down -** All of your goals should be written down somewhere. If you like the feel of a pen gliding across paper, put them in a notebook. If you're the type of person who likes to use sticky notes, grab your favorite post-it pad and jot them down. Personally, I record my goals electronically. I use my iPhone, iPad, laptop, text message reminders, etc. These are things I have with me on a regular basis that make it easy to access my goals from anywhere on any one of my devices. Use what works best for you.

If your goals are not written down, they aren't goals; they are just ideas. Ideas will stay ideas unless you put them in action. Penning your goals is putting them into action. Writing them down also allows you to be more efficient. Expressing your goals in the form of a positive statement is essential but being efficient is what will allow you to accomplish your goals. Once you've created a written action plan for your goals, you will be able to follow each of your accomplishments on the road to achieving them. This will allow you to build confidence in your ability to set and achieve goals. There is nothing more motivating than setting a goal and achieving it.

# HOW TO SET GOALS

## Different Types of Goals

Before I show you how to set goals, I first have to explain the different types of goals there are. You can set many kinds of goals. For the purpose of this book, we'll use three types of goals:

**Long-term Goals or Big Picture Goals** – These are goals that take a considerable amount of time to complete relative to your other goals. These can also be considered your dreams. Long-term goals typically aren't accomplished in one simple step. There is a journey to be taken to get there. A general timeframe for long-term goals is one to five years or greater.

**Intermediate Goals or Milestone Goals** – Typically, these are a series of steps or smaller goals that will take you to your ultimate destination. Milestone goals lead you to Big Picture Goals. A general timeframe for intermediate goals is six months to one year.

**Short-Term Goals or Mini Goals** – This kind of goal is used to breakdown your Milestone Goals. Short-term or mini goals allow you to manage your milestone goals. A general timeframe for short-term goals is one to six months.

I have developed this diagram to provide a visual for the different types of goals *Training Camp For Life* uses:

| Short-Term/ Mini Goals | → | Intermediate/ Milestone Goals | → | Long-Term/ Big Picture Goals |

## Goal-Setting Guide

*Training Camp For Life* has developed a goal-setting guide with you in mind. I intentionally created it to be simple, easy to understand, and easy to follow. Achieving your goals is not about what plan you use but more so about that you use a plan that works for you.

There are a lot of other goal-setting guides available. I would love to say that the *Training Camp For Life* guide will work for each and every reader but that's unrealistic. It will work for most but not all. Use what works for you. If this guide doesn't fit your needs, feel free to find something that does. If you Google "goal-setting guide" or "goal-setting plan" you will find many options to choose from.

"

**If your goals are not written down, they aren't goals; they are just ideas. Ideas stay ideas unless you put them into action.**

# TRAINING CAMP FOR LIFE'S GOAL-SETTING GUIDE

Now that you have some background information on goals and goal setting, you're ready to use the goal-setting guide. Instead of explaining the guide as I have done with the other information previously in this chapter, I decided to provide you with a copy of the goal-setting guide first. I will explain the details of this guide once you've looked it over. Here it is, the *Training Camp For Life* Goal-Setting Guide:

*Action Plan:*

## Training Camp For Life
## Goal-Setting Action Plan

Today's Date: _____

My Goal: (D.O. - I.T.) _____
_____

Type of Goal: _____ (short, intermediate, long)

Time Frame: _____ (1mo, 3mo, 6mo, 1yr, 3yr, 5yr)

Field of Goal: _____
(career, academic, education, sports, family, relationship, health, performance, big dream)

Benefits of Goal: _____
_____
_____

### State your goal in a positive statement:
_____

### Action Plan Steps:
Step 1: _____
Step 2: _____
Step 3: _____
Step 4: _____
Step 5: _____
(Use as many steps as you feel necessary to achieve your goal. Steps do not have to be in order.
Be sure to take steps that benefit the accomplishment of your goals.)

### Goal Milestones: (K.I.S.S.)
Milestone 1: _____ (1 Week/1 Month/1 Year)
Milestone 2: _____ (2 Weeks/2 Months/2 Years)
Milestone 3: _____ (3 Weeks/3 Months/3 Years)
Milestone 4: _____ (4 Weeks/4 Months/4 Years)
Milestone 5: _____ (5 Weeks/5 Months/5 Years)
Milestone 6: _____ (6 Weeks/6 Months/6 Years)
(Milestones are created to keep you on track to achieve your goal. They are set depending on the type of goal you set. If it is a short-term goal use weekly milestones. If it is an intermediate goal use months and for long-term goals use months and years. Use as many milestones necessary.)

### Personal Commitment:

I pledge to do what it takes to achieve my goal for the betterment of myself and those around me!

Signed: _____ Dated: _____
You must decide that your goal is worth the time, effort and dedication you will put into it.
You must also determine what your obstacles are in advance and decide to do whatever it takes to overcome those obstacles.

| All goals must be: S.M.A.R.T. | | | | |
|---|---|---|---|---|
| Specific | Measurable | Achievable | Realistic | Timeline |

Today's Date: **4/27/13**

**My Goal:(D.O. – I.T.)** Sale over 100,000 copies of "Training Camp For Life"

**Type of Goal:** Intermediate (short, intermediate, long)

**Time Frame:** 3 years  (1mo, 3mo, 6mo, 1yr, 3yr, 5yr)

**Field of Goal:** Personal/Career – Author & Speaker
(career, academic, education, sports, family, relationship, personal, health, performance, big dream etc.)

**Benefits of Goal: 1.** Impacting the lives of young men all over the world.
      **2.** Empowering young men with tools to see success in athletics
        and in life.
      **3.** Become a best selling author and effective inspirational
        speaker.

### State your goal in a positive statement:

I will sale over 100,000 copies of "Training Camp For Life"!!!
I am a best selling author and effective inspirational speaker!!!

### Action Plan Steps:
**Step 1:** Write one chapter a week
**Step 2:** Build my support team: Agent, manager, administrative assistant, event coordinator
**Step 3:** Contact Potential Book Tour Sponsors: Sponsor the Training Camp For Life Book Tour
**Step 4:** Contact key personnel at High Schools, Colleges, Faith Based & Nonprofit Organizations
**Step 5:** Go on a Nationwide Book Tour: Minimum of 10 States, 25 Colleges/Churches/High Schools

**Goal Milestones: (K.I.S.S.)**

**Milestone 1:** Find the right book publishing company  - 3 Months
**Milestone 2:** Have book release day event -  6 Months
**Milestone 3:** Sale books on iTunes - 6 Months
**Milestone 4:** Go on my first book tour – 1 Year
**Milestone 5:** Appear on Oprah and have "TCFL" in Oprah's Book Club – 3 Years
(Milestones are created to keep you on track to achieve your goal. They are set depending on the type of goal you set. If it is a short-term goal use weekly milestones. If it is an intermediate goal use months and for long-term goals use months and years. Use as many milestones necessary.)

### Personal Commitment:

I pledge to do what it takes to achieve my goal for the betterment of myself and those around me!

**Signed:**                            **Dated: 4/27/13**
You must decide that your goal is worth the time, effort and dedication you will put into it.
You must also determine what your obstacles are in advance and decide to do whatever it takes to overcome those obstacles.

All goals must be: S.M.A.R.T.
Specific    Measurable    Achievable    Realistic    Timeline

I've provided you with an example that guides you through the action plan. I followed the steps and filled in the blanks. Feel free to use my example as a starting point to get you on your way but at some point, I want you to make this personal and specific to your own goals and what you want to accomplish in life.

My objective is to get you setting and achieving your goals early in life so that you can make this a habit, as this is one of the best habits you can ever have. You WILL achieve your goals if you follow this action plan and use the tools *Training Camp For Life* has provided you with. The only thing that can stop you from achieving your goals is YOU! You are the most important person in your life right now. If you don't help yourself now, you won't be able to help anyone else in the future.

It's time for you to become selfish. Yes, SELFISH! Hear me out on this one. There are two types of selfishness, bad selfishness and good selfishness. Bad selfishness is when you want things for yourself for all the wrong reasons. On the other hand, good selfishness is when you want things for yourself for good reasons. It's OK to be selfish at this point in time in your life.

Now, don't go out and say, "Steve Sanders told me to be selfish," and take advantage of what I'm telling you in a negative way. I'm saying that it's OK to be selfish for good reasons right now. Focus on yourself and achieving your goals. Take advantage of the time you have as a young man because if you miss this moment, you'll never be able to get it back. The things you do now will mold and shape your future and the person you become. The habits you create and behaviors you carry out will start to solidify the values you live by. Be the person you want to become now. Follow this action plan and you will become that person you always wanted to be!

## Routinely Review Your Action Plan

Now that you have one (or more) action plan(s) completed, it is crucial that you routinely review your plan. You will need to look at your plan daily, weekly, and monthly as a reminder of what you committed yourself to. Routinely reviewing your plan will also help keep your goals fresh in your mind. The more you're thinking about them, the more you're thinking about how you plan to accomplish them.

With modern technology you can have your action plans with you 24/7. I save my action plan to my iBooks app on my iPhone, and as my screen saver. I also set alarms and reminders that show me my goals. You can do this with any smartphone. If you're more of a paper person, find a nice notebook or as I said earlier, use sticky notes. Place little reminders in places you frequently visit like your bathroom, car, nightstand, dresser, locker, or even your school notebooks. Many of you probably already do these types of things. Now it's time to take it to the next level. This action plan is going to change how you set and achieve goals.

## Dream Big!!!

Let your imagination soar! Dream of things that you always wanted to accomplish in life. The last thing that is limiting you from reaching your goals is your lack of imagination. It's time for you to take off the invisible chains that have been holding you in bondage too long. You are free from doubt, fear, worry, let-downs, low self-esteem, low self-confidence, and any other negative mindset that has haunted you in the past.

It's time to dream big! You are going to reach levels you've never even imagined you would. Get excited! I'm excited for you and this new journey you're about to embark on. You've already taken the first step. Now let's put your plan in motion and start seeing some results. The choice is yours. Start setting and achieving your goals today.

# BECOMING A PRO-FESSIONAL

9

**"Commitment is a big part of what I am and what I believe. How committed are you to winning? How committed are you to being a good friend? To being trustworthy? To being successful? How committed are you to being a good father, a good teammate, a good role model? There's that moment every morning when you look in the mirror: Are you committed, or are you not?"**

– LeBron James

Now that we have the informative things out the way, let's get to the real stuff you want to hear.

Something tells me that you are reading this book because you want an edge on the competition. You're looking for something, anything that will give you a leg up on the next guy. Well, if that's you then this is your chapter. You say you want to go pro? I feel you, man...

When I was a kid all I ever dreamed of was playing professional sports. I wanted to go the League so bad I could taste it. I just knew I was going to get there somehow, some way. By the time I was fourteen years old I was pretty much a standout in every sport I played. I won championships, received MVP trophies, earned gold medals, and got just about anything else that was associated with finishing on top. Everywhere I went I had a ball in my hand. I wore athletic gear pretty much every day, even if it meant wearing gym shorts underneath my clothes. I was always ready to play.

People used to say to me, "Do you think you're going to the League?" My reply would always be, "I already made it to the League; I just have to grow up." Yeah, I was a little cocky back then. But that's what I believed and I didn't have a problem expressing it to anyone.

Many of you young guys reading this book feel the same way; you know you're going pro. You can feel it in your soul. You dream about it. You eat, breathe, and sleep your sport. There is nothing wrong with that. In fact, that's a good thing. Keep doing that. Value your confidence in yourself, because there are a lot of people who wish they were that confident in something. If you're not that kind of person or if you're not as confident in your abilities, don't feel bad. Maybe you don't know if you're good enough to go to the League. That's OK too. My goal in this chapter is to get you to understand what it means to become a **pro**fessional and what it takes to go pro whether you feel like you have what it takes or not.

Before we get to what it takes to go pro I need to tell you a little about my own professional career. This isn't to brag or boast about my successes at all. I'm more likely to tell you about what I have done wrong to this point than what I have done right. I am not the hero in this story.

I love sports. I am what you would call a sports head. I will pretty much watch any game with a ball nowadays. I haven't always been this way. Over the years I developed a love and respect for sports outside of the three most popular ones (football, basketball, and baseball). One of those sports is golf. I used to think golf wasn't a sport. I used to say, "Golf isn't a sport. It's just something old guys do because they can't play real sports anymore."

Yeah... That's what I used to say until I played eighteen holes for the first time. One of my mentors heard me making my little joke about the game and he invited me to play with him one weekend. I took him up on the offer because I wanted to prove a point to him. Well, let's just say by the ninth hole of golf I was drenched in sweat, tired, hot, and ready to go home. My mentor looks over at me and says very calmly, "Who's the old man now?" I thought I was proving a point to him and the entire time he was proving his point to me.

After that day, my level of respect for the game of golf was much greater. I didn't understand the amount of focus, precision, strength, and endurance a person needs to play the game. I assumed it was easy and anyone would be able to do it. As I matured and worked on my golf game, I saw that it took just the same amount of great work ethic—if not more—to become a good golfer as it does to become great in other more physically challenging sports.

Maybe golf isn't your game. It sure wasn't mine. That's OK. Whatever your game is, to perform at a professional level you're going to have to put in some serious work. You have to have a great work ethic. For most athletes, you won't even be able to count the amount of hours you put in. Others may not have to put in as much due to their God-given ability. The one question you have to ask yourself in sports is, "How bad do you want it?"

If you've played any type of sport and been around a good coach who pushes you to achieve more, you've heard someone ask, "How bad do you want it?" Most good coaches won't allow players to get stuck. Whether it's a poorly performing team or a team that wins the championship every year, a good coach always pushes their players to work harder, give more effort, and do their absolute best. For a team, following these principles are the staples to success.

## Work Ethic

It Ain't Over, Till It's Over

As I mentioned previously, I am a big sports fan. Currently, I'm watching the 2013 NBA Finals, the Miami Heat versus San Antonio Spurs. Without question, this series will go down as one of the greatest NBA Finals of all time. The series is tied 3-3 and

"

It's not about the moment, it's about the preparation for the moment.

Game 7 is a couple of days away. Game 6 was amazing! I haven't watched a game with that much intensity in a long time.

With the championship on the line and less than thirty seconds left in regulation, the Heat were down by five points and needed to pull out a miracle to win this game. Fans began to leave the arena and social media sites were crowning the Spurs as champions. But if you know anything about sports you know *it ain't over until it's over!*

In order to send the game into overtime where the Heat would eventually win, they had two big three-pointers from LeBron James and Ray Allen. LeBron's three-pointer was from deep. He's the reigning MVP for a reason. When the game is on the line, he steps to the challenge head on and gives it his all.

Ray Allen, the NBA's all-time leading three-point shooter, hit the biggest shot of the game. With just five seconds left on the clock. The ball was kicked out to him by Chris Bosh and Ray Allen, in his iconic corner of the three-point line hits the game tying three. Needless to say, the game was really intense.

After I calmed myself from jumping up and down in my house like a little kid, I began to think about the amount of work ethic Ray Allen has put in just to make one shot. Most people would argue that it wasn't just for one shot but I beg to differ and I think Ray Allen would too. Let's think about this for a second.

Ray Allen was signed by the Miami Heat in the off-season because he is a great shooter, the greatest of all-time. His purpose on the team is to shoot. With the game on the line, he pulls up and hits the biggest shot of his career. Ray Allen has made big shots in his career before but this was the NBA Finals in a win-or-GO-HOME situation. Let's not forget to mention that Allen is in his sixteenth season and may retire after this year. The point is, he made a huge shot that everyone will remember.

But I think a little differently. While everyone else couldn't believe he hit such an amazing shot, I was thinking about the amount of work he's put in just for that one moment. Everyone has the moment in the backyard or at the park when you're playing with your crew or by yourself. What do you do? You start counting down...5-4-3-2-1 and you shoot the ball imagining you're playing in a championship game.

Ray Allen is well known for his work ethic. It's rumored that he shoots a minimum of 100 free throws a day. He must have shot millions of practice shots in the gym preparing for this moment.

I believe he expected to hit that shot. I'm sure he's humble and won't tell you that he knew he was going to hit the shot but his actions speak louder than his words. His actions of shooting hundreds of shots a day just to prepare and be ready for this one moment says he expected to make the shot.

OK, make your point, Steve! The point is this: your work ethic prepares you for the unknown. The things you do now to prepare for that "one big moment" will determine whether you will hit "the big shot." It's not about the moment, it's about the preparation for the moment. What you do in the dark will come to light. What do I mean by that? I'm glad you asked.

The things you do in the dark are the things you do to prepare that no one else sees. Maybe it's the late night runs you go for, the extra reps completed on the bench. Maybe it's the team meeting you called to refocus your players or the extra time you spend watching film on yourself or an upcoming opponent. Whatever you do that no one else sees will eventually be put on display for everyone to see, good or bad. So, if you do nothing, everyone will see nothing. If you prepare, everyone will see the fruit of your labor. Not only will they see the fruit, they will be able to enjoy the fruit as well.

# CHAPTER 10

# SURROUND YOURSELF WITH AN ALL-STAR ROSTER OF SUPPORT

# 10

**"The way a team plays as a whole determines its success. You may have the greatest bunch of individual stars in the world, but if they don't play together, the club won't be worth a dime."**

- Babe Ruth (One of the Greatest Baseball Players Ever)

I was recently reading a blog called *413 Ways to Become Successful* and I came across an interesting article. It was titled "Surround Yourself with an All-Start Roster of Support." The article motivated me to write this section on how to build a supportive team. Why do you need a supportive team? Because no one reaches accomplishments alone in life. Everyone needs the support of others around them. In business, people network. They exchange business cards to later discuss ideas and to see if there is an opportunity for them to partner with each other.

You have heard the expression, "It's not what you know, it's who you know." I added a few words to that statement years ago by saying it's also "who knows you." Most people are willing to help people they know or know of. But what if you already had a team of support around you? Maybe you do but just aren't aware of it yet. The following is a recommendation of how to surround yourself with an All-Star Roster of Support:

## On Offense

In any sport you play, the offensive objective is to score! Everyone knows that. In football, the objective for the offense is to score points in the form of touchdowns or field goals. When you're building your all-star roster of support, your offensive objective is to accomplish your goals, soak up as much knowledge as possible from each individual, and apply the knowledge you obtain in the necessary areas of your life.

## Your Backfield

**The Quarterback** – The quarterback position in football is arguably the most important position in all of sports. The quarterback calls the shots, makes the decisions, and is the leader of the offensive. The "quarterback" of your all-star roster is the leader. This person ultimately will make the final choice on every decision. This person is YOU! You are the quarterback of your all-star roster. We are all our own leaders at the end of the day and we have to decide to lead our lives in such a way that directs us to the "end zone of success."

**The Running Back** – The running back (RB) position is very important to the offense as well. A running back plays a lot of roles. Oftentimes, the RB carries the workload by running the ball. In addition to running the ball, one of the running back's most important jobs is to protect the quarterback. He has to see his blindside, scan the perimeter, and block any defender that makes it past the front line.

The running back is your closest friend. This is a person that is in the backfield with you and sees things from your viewpoint. They will tell you when things are coming that you don't see. They will help carry the workload in areas of your life where you may need to lean on someone for help. Your running back is your running mate. For some, this may be a serious girlfriend or even a brother, sister, cousin, or mentor. Most of you might already have a running back on your roster.

**Offensive Line –** Also known as the "big boys." These guys are the first line of protection. They too keep the quarterback safe. But unlike the running back position, their only job is to protect the quarterback. The offensive line doesn't always get as much credit as they deserve.

The offensive line in your life are those who protect you. They keep you safe from hurt, harm, and danger. They keep a roof over your head, clothes on you back, and food on the table. They pray for you, which also protects you from things you can't see. Without a doubt the offensive line on your all-star roster of support are your parental guardians. I say parental guardians because in today's society, we have many types of families, meaning your biological mother and father may or may not be the ones who provide for and protect you every day. It could be your grandparents, your father and stepmother, or an older brother. There are blended families, foster families, church

TRAINING CAMP FOR LIFE

families and many other types of families. Your offensive line is made up of your guardians, the people who look after you and love you unconditionally with all of their heart.

## Skill Positions

**Wide Receiver –** The wide receiver position is designated for playmakers. They are usually known as your skill players. They make big plays by catching the football and advancing it down the field in big yards.

On your roster, your wide receivers will be people you can count on to make "big plays" for you. Maybe this is a person who is always there for you in your time of need or a person who you go to for encouragement or advice. This position differs a little from the rest because you may not know this person directly. It could be someone you follow on a social site who is uplifting, motivating, and inspiring.

This would be a great place on your roster for a mentor. Mentors help you see places that you don't and get you in positions you wouldn't be able to on your own. Jay Z said, "A midget standing on the shoulders of a giant can see much further than a giant."

We should all have people around us whose shoulders we stand on. Most might argue that the wide receiver position on your roster is your Most Valuable Player (MVP). I'm not just saying that because I played wide receiver in the NFL either. Just take a

"

A midget standing
on the shoulders of
a giant can see
much further than a
giant.

– Jay Z

look at great organizations such as Big Brothers, Big Sisters and the Boys and Girls Club. Their sole purpose is to provide mentors to young people who need them and to expose them to opportunities, professions, activities, and people they wouldn't normally have access to on their own. Everyone should have a mentor of some sort.

## The Coach

Options to consider for your coach (or coaching staff) range from your mom or dad, stepparents, or grandparents to the actual coaches who coach the team you play for. More than likely this person will have more experience in life than you will depending on the stage you're at in your life. This is the reason you allow them to lead you and you follow their direction. There are so many different types of coaches. Traditionally, you have sports coaches of course but you also have life coaches. Life coaches are professionals that specialize in certain areas of expertise. I am a certified life coach as you have seen on the cover of the book. My areas of expertise are leadership, goal-setting, athletics, pursuing success and personal growth.

No matter how great you are, everyone has a coach. Tiger Woods is one of the greatest golfers of all-time. Tiger still has a golf coach. The same goes for players like Peyton Manning, Tom Brady, Kevin Durant and any other superstar you see. They all have someone they trust to advise them in their profession.

# Intro To Part II

**"Never give up! Failure and rejection are only the first step to succeeding."**

- Jimmy Valvano's 1993 Inspirational ESPY Speech

As I mentioned in the beginning of the book, *Developing Champions In Sports and In Life* is a three-part series. Part I sets the framework for where you are headed. Its purpose is to lay the foundation for your future. If you follow the practical steps in Part I, you will be ready to move on to Part II and take the next steps toward becoming a true champion in sports and in life.

Part II of *Developing Champions In Sports And In Life* takes a more in-depth approach to addressing the challenges young student-athletes are facing on a daily basis. In it, I'll share my testimony, the testimony of some of your favorite athletes, and even some of your peers who I have met in the process of writing Part I.

With chapter titles such as "Got Purpose?", "Training For A Change", "The **TRUE** Definition of a Man", and "The Dash" just to name a few, Part II is going to really answer a lot of the unaddressed questions you may have in life. As young men, we deal with an abundance of issues on a daily basis. Most of us have questions but no one to talk to about them. If you have ever felt this way, Part II will be for you.

I remember when I was in college and I couldn't read. I did everything possible to hide the fact that I needed help. I didn't want to show weakness. I didn't want people to laugh at me. I spent a great deal of time and energy covering up my struggle. It wasn't until I reached out to my college coach, Zach Azzanni, that I received the help I needed. I was fed up hiding the fact that I couldn't read. I was tired of walking out of class when it was my turn to read. I didn't want to feel ashamed anymore. So I shared my issue with my coach. Coach Z and his wife immediately made me feel comfortable. Without hesitation, they helped me. I will share these stories and much more in detail throughout Part II of this series.

Someone reading this closing chapter may have the same issue I struggled with. Or maybe you have abandonment issues or are even struggling with your identity. Whatever your issue is, there is someone willing and ready to help you. You just have to overcome the fear of reaching out when you're in need.

Fair warning, Part II will be deep. I am going to really depict and debunk topics and issues that have hindered young men and older men for generations. I'm excited to go on this journey with you after you have finished Part I.

Lastly, it is my sincere prayer that this book has been a blessing to you both in your sports life and daily walk. I am genuinely grateful for every reader who decided to pick up *Training Camp For Life – Developing Champions In Sports and In Life*. When I began writing this book, I was fearful of the unknown. "I'm not a great writer." "Who will read the book?" "How will I publish it with no money?" These were all my worries.

But God! I stayed faithful throughout and I trusted the process. As my pastor, Dr. R.A. Vernon would say, "I GET TO SERVE." *Training Camp For Life* is so much more than a book or organization; it is a ministry. I truly believe that if we follow God's will for our lives, we will walk in purpose and be fulfilled with joy and love.

Every day I wake up I am so grateful that I get to **inspire**, **impact**, and **influence** the lives of millions of young athletes across the world. I **get to** do what I love to do and can I tell you something? I am having a ball doing it.

Until next time… Live life **INSPIRED**, make an **IMPACT**, and be a great **INFLUENCE**!

# Steve Sanders Bio

Steve Sanders was born and raised in Cleveland, Ohio where he attended East High School. He was an All-State football and basketball player, and an All-American track performer for the historic Blue Bombers. Steve continued his education at Bowling Green State University where he played for the future hall of fame coach Urban Meyer. He finished his career at BGSU with impressive career stats of 156 receptions for 2,324 yards and 24 touchdowns. More importantly, he graduated college with a degree in Political Science. Sanders on field success led him to play in the NFL for his hometown, the Cleveland Browns, during the 2006-2008 seasons. He also played for the Detroit Lions and Arizona Cardinals in 2009-2010.

As part of his life commitment to directly impacting young people who have come from similar environments and socioeconomics as he has, in 2011, Sanders willingly walked away from the NFL. In that same year he announced the opening of The Steve Sanders Academy, an Ohio Community School in his old community. At the age of 28, Sanders was one of the youngest people across the country to found an educational institution. He is also one of the first professional athletes to willingly step away from his childhood dream of playing a professional sport to commit his life to directly impacting youth by opening a charter school.

In addition to his playing career and philanthropy, Steve Sanders recently launched Training Camp For Life, a motivational speaking platform and nonprofit organization created to inspire, impact and influence student-athletes in all aspects of sports and life. With his unique speaking style and relatable story, Sanders is able to grasp many different types of audiences. His new book "Training Camp For Life: Developing Champions In Sports and In Life" is set to release May 1, 2014. Steve Sanders will begin the Training Camp For Life Book Tour in summer 2014.

# TRAINING CAMP FOR LIFE

Also available on ebook.

Download your digital copy *NOW!*

Visit www.**TrainingCampForLife**.org

# BOOK
# STEVE SANDERS

Are you in need of a *relevant* and *effective speaker?*

Book ***Steve Sanders*** as your Keynote Speaker for your next Major Event

## CONTACT US AT:

info@TrainingCampForLife.org *or*

visit www.TrainingCampForLife.org for booking details